Cover illustration: The increasing commitment of US ships to active roles in the Atlantic came rapidly after July 1941. On 16 September US Navy ships were ordered to aid the Royal Canadian Navy in escorting all convoys between North America and a mid-ocean point south of Iceland. This led to the permanent basing of two old battleships and two cruisers at Hvalfjord, Iceland, in mid-September to establish the White Patrol, assigned the task of patrolling the Denmark Strait. *Idaho* (BB-42), one of the White Patrol battleships, is seen here at Hvalfjord, 2 October 1941. She wears Measure 12 camouflage. (USN)

1. The aircraft carrier *Hornet* (CV-8) at Pearl Harbor in May 1942. Note the FD radar on her Mk. 37 high-angle directors above the bridge and abaft the funnel: this was a new fire-control system for anti-aircraft guns. (USN)

WARSHIPS ILLUSTRATED No 10

The US Navy
in
World War Two

1941–1942 ROBERT C. STERN

ARMS AND ARMOUR PRESS

Introduction

First published in Great Britain in 1987 by Arms and
Armour Press Ltd., Link House, West Street, Poole,
Dorset BH15 1LL.

Distributed in the USA by Sterling Publishing Co.
Inc., 2 Park Avenue, New York, NY 10016.

Distributed in Australia by
Capricorn Link (Australia) Pty. Ltd.,
P.O. Box 665, Lane Cove, New South Wales 2066.

British Library Cataloguing in Publication data:
Stern, Robert C.
The US Navy in World War Two, 1941–1942.
(Warships illustrated; 10)
1. United States. *Navy* – History
2. Warships – United States – History –
20th century
I. Title II. Series
623.8'25'0973 VA58

ISBN 0-85368-759-5

Edited and designed by Roger Chesneau; typeset by
Typesetters (Birmingham) Ltd.; printed and bound
in Italy in association with Keats European
Production Ltd., London.

2
North Carolina (BB-55) began working up in the
Atlantic in May 1941. The photograph probably
dates from the time of the Pearl Harbor attack,
because the battleship carries a radar antenna,
CXAM-1, on her foremast. She is still being painted
up in Measure 1 – note the unpainted deck to the left.
(USN)

The US Navy found itself in a shooting war rather abruptly on
the morning of 7 December 1941. This story, however, begins
well before that, as the United States edged ever closer to
involvement in the crucial Battle of the Atlantic. Unwilling to
stand by and watch Great Britain succumb to the U-boat
threat, yet politically restrained from declaring war, President
Franklin D. Roosevelt instituted a 'short of war' policy
designed gradually to increase US involvement without unduly
alarming the isolationist majority in America. The Japanese
attack on Pearl Harbor instantly solved his political problems,
but created the worst kind of military nightmare. The US
faced a two-front conflict spread over more than half the globe.
At first, the only force available to fight that war was the Navy,
damaged but not crippled, obliged to carry on the fight with
the resources available.

This volume is the first in a planned multi-volume series
dealing with the US Navy in the Second World War. It covers
the prewar 'short of war' period, the Pearl Harbor attack, the
early war involvement in the Atlantic and the crucial South and
Central Pacific campaigns that concluded with the Battles of
the Coral Sea and Midway. This is a period of slightly less than
a year, from late June 1941, when 'FDR' declared an
'Unlimited National Emergency' and took over the task of
escorting convoys between the US and Iceland, to early June
1942. It will mention climates and locales as diverse as
Reykjavik and Bora Bora.

The task of compiling a photographic essay covering this
fascinating period is almost as complex and interesting as the
story itself. In general, naval warfare is harder to document
pictorially than war on the ground or in the air, since actions
are much more likely to take place in poor visibility or at night
(in fact, one of the most decisive campaigns of the war, the
battle for the mastery of the waters around Guadalcanal, took
place almost exclusively at night), and participants are often
spread out over vast areas of water and air, mere specks on the
horizon at best. Add to this an administrative quirk that put
the vast bulk of the photographic resources in the hands of
BuAer (the Navy's Bureau of Aeronautics) at the beginning of
the war, and it is surprising that there emerged a rich and
complete photographic archive.

The author wishes to acknowledge the help of those people
without whom he never would have been able to find his way
through this maze of archives and collections. These include
Chuck Haberlein and his staff at the Naval Historical Center,
Bob Cressman (who among his other accomplishments is
Carrier Editor of *The Hook*), the helpful folk at the Air Force's
Magazine and Book Division and the research staff at the
Smithsonian Institution's Air and Space Museum, particularly
my friend Dana Bell. Without them and many others, this
book could never have come to pass.
                                                    Robert C. Stern

▲3

3. The action in the first year of the US Navy's war stretched across half the globe, taking place in climates ranging from tropical to frigid. The latter extreme is shown here in this view of *Gleaves* (DD-423) playing icebreaker at Argentia, 27 February 1942. In common with many other Atlantic destroyers, *Gleaves* was heavily involved in the war well before Pearl Harbor. At this time she was part of TG.4.1, providing escort for HX and ON convoys. (USN)

4. The US Navy certainly had no excuse for being surprised by the idea behind the Japanese carrier raid on Pearl Harbor. During several of the annual Fleet Problems during the 1930s, the big

carriers *Saratoga* (CV-3) and *Lexington* (CV-2) had carried out surprise air assaults on land targets. This was particularly true of the 1938 exercise, when *Saratoga* carried out a raid on Pearl Harbor, approaching the island unobserved from the north-west. This photograph shows the two carriers together off Waikiki Beach, with Diamond Head in the background, after the 1933 exercise. So similar were the two vessels that a large black stripe on the funnel was used to help pilots tell *Saratoga* (with the stripe) from her sister ship. (USAF)

▼4

5. One of the first acts of Roosevelt's 'short of war' strategy was the exchange with Churchill of fifty First World War destroyers for bases to several British Western Hemisphere bases, formalized on 2 September 1940. The swap helped Britain, which badly needed extra hulls of any kind to help stem the U-boat tide and which greatly appreciated the US Navy's taking over of the responsibility for guarding Argentia and Bermuda; for the United States, it was a tentative first step towards engagement in the Atlantic. This photograph shows one of several storage sites for the old 'four-pipers'. (USN)

6. The US Navy's involvement in the Atlantic began to increase considerably after 8 July 1941, when the Icelandic government somewhat reluctantly 'invited' the United States to take over the defence of the island from the British; more importantly, Washington at the same time unilaterally announced that the US Navy would be taking over the responsibility for protecting all convoys between the USA and Iceland. While US ships were ordered not to take offensive action against any belligerents, they were empowered to defend themselves. One of the first units committed to escort duty on the US–Iceland route was *Long Island* (ACV-1, later CVE-1), the first of the long line of escort carriers that would win the Battle of the Atlantic. At the forward edge of the short flight deck (later lengthened) are two F2A Buffaloes of VS-201. (USN)

▲7　▼8

The flagship of the Atlantic Fleet was *Augusta* (CA-31), seen here at Bermuda, September 1941. She had carried Roosevelt to the Atlantic Charter meeting with Churchill in August. She wears a new Measure 12 graded camouflage, composed of horizontal bands of Sea Blue, Ocean Gray and Haze Gray; the latter two colours were hard to tell apart. This scheme could be distinguished from the later Measure 22 by the fact that the division between tones on the hull followed the sheer line rather than the horizon. Note the very early radar set, CXAM-1, on the foremast. (USN)

The White Patrol battleship *Mississippi* (BB-41), seen at Hvalfjord 4 October 1941; like *Idaho* (see cover illustration), she is painted in Measure 12. Because the ship is backlit in this view, it is difficult to distinguish the darker colours on the hull, but the division between the Ocean Gray and Haze Gray on the bridge superstructure can be plainly seen. (USN via Bob Cressman)

Other old battleships were based at the North American end of the US–Iceland route. This photograph shows *Texas* (BB-35) at Prentice Bay, Newfoundland, 14 October 1941. Her camouflage scheme is very light in appearance, making it likely that this is an example of the rarely used Measure 3 Light Gray system intended for misty environments. Note the CXAM-1 sea search radar on the foremast. (USN)

10, 11. It was inevitable that putting US ships between U-boats and targets would cause an 'incident'. After several near-misses, just such occurred when a torpedo from *U-568* hit *Kearny* (DF-432) square amidships on October 1941 during a night-long battle to protect convoy SC.48. *Kearny* limped back to Reykjavik, where she is seen on 19 October along with *Monssen* (DD-436). Both new destroyers and the older 'four-pipers' in the background wear Measure 12 camouflage, which called for Sea Blue up to the sheer line of the main deck. For ships with forecastle decks, like *Kearny*, this meant that part of the hull was painted Ocean Gray; for flush-decked ships like the older destroyers, the entire hull was painted the darker colour. (NHC)

9▲

10▲ 11▼

▲12

12, 13. Another consequence of the increasingly aggressive US position was the Odenwald Incident on 6 November 1941. The old light cruiser *Omaha* (CL-4) caught up with the German blockade-runner *Odenwald* off the coast of Brazil and captured her without a fight. *Omaha* wears the short-lived Measure 1 camouflage. This scheme was soon abandoned because it was too dark (note how much more visible *Omaha* is than *Odenwald*, which is painted a lighter grey) and too neutral in tone (bluer greys provided much better camouflage). (NHC)

▼13

14▲

14. Even with the as-yet undeclared war being waged on the mid-Atlantic convoy routes, the Western Atlantic was a safe place for new ships to work up. Thus *North Carolina* (BB-55) took advantage of the quiet waters to run through her trials late in 1941. She wears Measure 1 with Measure 5, a false bow wave painted in white. *North Carolina* was intended to join the Atlantic Fleet but was transferred to the Pacific soon after Pearl Harbor.

15. The merits and morality of the 'short of war' strategy have been debated ever since 1945. Whether it is seen as a cynical attempt to force an unwilling nation into a war that was not its concern or a highly moral stance in the face of a slumbering populace depends entirely on the viewer's perspective. What is certain is that, before late November 1941, no one really expected the war for America to start in the Pacific rather than the Atlantic – and even after intelligence clearly showed Japanese movements toward Malaya at the beginning of December, no one seriously considered the possibility that six aircraft carriers would be bearing down on Pearl Harbor from the stormy North Pacific, ready to launch at first light on 7 December 1941. (NASM)

15▼

▲16   ▼17

16. From the Japanese point of view, the attack on Pearl Harbor was a 'textbook' exercise. The complete surprise achieved by the initial wave of torpedo-bombers meant that at first there was no aerial opposition and very little defensive ground fire. Attacking aircraft wheeled over their targets, lining up their release with incredible accuracy. This photograph was taken very early in the attack. The water spout in the centre is from *Oklahoma* (BB-37), just hit by one of the five or more torpedoes that led to her rapid capsizing. Ford Island dominates the centre of the photograph, which looks towards the north-east. Ten-Ten Dock is to the right, with the submarine base behind. (NHC)

17. Another aerial view, taken at nearly the same moment as the previous photograph, shows 'Battleship Row' under torpedo attack. From the left, the ships are *Nevada* (BB-36), *Arizona* (BB-39) with the minelayer *Oglala* (CM-4) outboard, *Tennessee* (BB-43) with *West Virginia* (BB-48) outboard, *Maryland* (BB-46) with *Oklahoma* (BB-37) outboard, the oiler *Neosho* (AO-23) and *California* (BB-44). The

initial torpedo attack was by far the most devastating, and the most vulnerable ships are already showing signs of sinking. *California* is down at the bow, while *Oklahoma* and *West Virginia* have noticeable lists. Hickam Field, an Army Air Corps base, burns in the background. (NHC)

18. The second phase of the attack was by horizontal bombers, again torpedo-bombers, armed with converted armour-piercing shells. 'Battleship Row' from *Nevada* on the left to *Neosho* on the right is visible. The latter vessel is still undamaged. *Arizona* has just taken the first of the bomb hits that would sink her, whilst *West Virginia* and *Oklahoma* both show signs of sinking. (NHC)

19. A few minutes later, the damage caused by the attack of the horizontal bombers is evident. *Nevada* is still unscathed, but *Arizona* has been hit and burns fiercely. *West Virginia* and *Tennessee* are mostly obscured by smoke from *Arizona*. The hull of *Oklahoma*, now capsized, is visible at the right. (NHC)

▲20 ▼21

0. Alone at the head of 'Battleship Row', *California* was in a particularly vulnerable position. She was hit by two torpedoes in the initial attack and began to list noticeably. The second torpedo hit abreast 'B' turret, causing her to settle by the bow. The smoke seemingly rising from *California* actually comes from the more heavily damaged battleships further up 'Battleship Row'. The flag seen at the top left of this photograph betrays the stiff wind that was to cause the abandonment of the ship. (USN)

1. Seen a short while later from one of the concrete moorings at Berth Fox-2, *California* continues to list to port. Only the combined effects of the strong mooring cables over the starboard side now stretched nearly taut and rapid counterflooding kept her from capsizing later that day. For unknown reasons, she is flying a profusion of signal flags from her foremast yardarms. The tanker *Neosho*, docked at the Gasoline Wharf, is clearly visible in the background, and the hull of the capsized *Oklahoma* is visible just to the right of *Neosho*. (USN)

. This view from Ford Island looks down 'Battleship Row' soon after the attackers departed. *California* continues to heel slightly to port. *Maryland*, just to the right of the huge smoke cloud coming from *Arizona*, was the least damaged of the battleships along Ford Island. To her right are *West Virginia*, which sank in an upright position, and the capsized *Oklahoma*. (USN)

. The danger of burning oil was very real. The stiff tradewind blew the oil down on *California*, leading to the order to abandon ship. Note the men swarming down the mooring cables to the concrete quay. They then had to swim a short distance to the small boat wharf at the left. Had *California* not had to be abandoned, she would probably not have sunk, but without a crew on board to fight the flooding she settled on the bottom during the afternoon. (USN)

22 ▲   23 ▼

▲24   ▼25

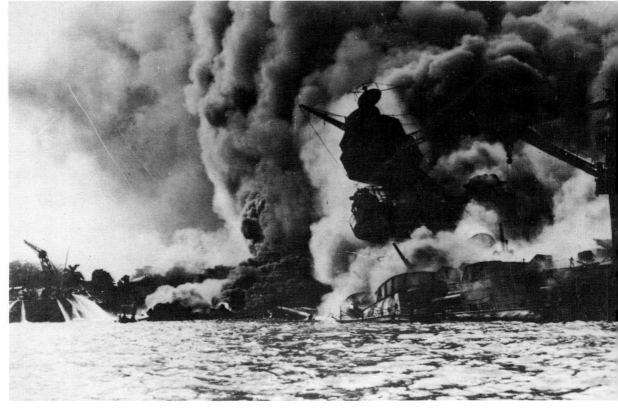

24. The most spectacular, and deadly, single event on 7 December was the explosion of *Arizona*'s forward magazine. Hit by an armour-piercing bomb dropped by one of the horizontal bombers, she was literally torn in half just forward of the conning tower. Her destruction was signalled by a huge plume of black smoke. (USN)

25. The explosion caused *Arizona*'s foremast to collapse forward towards the hole where 'B' turret used to be. The cloud of dense black smoke pouring from her fires is visible in virtually every photograph of Pearl Harbor that day. The crew of *Tennessee*, to the left, poured water over her stern in an unsuccessful attempt to keep the intense heat of *Arizona*'s fires from damaging *Tennessee*'s stern plates. (USN)

26. A prewar view of *Trippe* (DD-403). Despite the backlighting, it is possible to distinguish the standard peacetime paint scheme used by the US Navy – overall Standard Navy Gray (a very light bluish grey) with black funnel top. The bow numerals are large, in white and with black shadows. (USN)

27. The transition to camouflage began with the distribution of instructions on nine basic schemes in January 1941. As always, compliance with such instructions was uneven, and ships were camouflaged only when their scheduled refits came around. In this view of five Pacific Fleet destroyers at Pearl Harbor, mid-1941, *Clark* (DD-361) is the closest to the camera. Three of the ships (including *Clark*) wear the new Measure 1, Dark Gray up to the line of the top of the funnel and Light Gray above that (the colours were pure neutral greys); the other two ships are still in peacetime colours. (USN)

28. Measure 1 was considered to be highly effective camouflage against both surface and aerial observation, and from this angle that seemed a reasonable conclusion. *Drayton* (DD-366) was active in the Pacific in the early days of the war, being part of TF.11, *Lexington*'s battle group. Note the chrome yellow upper wing surfaces of the Navy aircraft from which this photograph was taken. (USN)

26 ▲

27 ▲   28 ▼

▲ 29

29, 30. Two views of *Minneapolis* (CA-36) at Pearl Harbor early in the war. She wears Measure 11, one of the 'second generation' camouflage schemes introduced in September 1941. These new schemes differed from the first batch primarily in using purple-greys instead of neutral tones. The illustrations demonstrate why caution must be used when Second World War colour photograph are assessed. Measure 11 was an overall Sea Blue scheme intended as the replacement for Measure 1, but the first of these views is markedly too yellow, the second slightly too red. The correct rendition of Sea Blue lies somewhere in between. (USN)

▼ 30

1. Continuing the scene at Pearl Harbor, *Tennessee* was jammed in place between *West Virginia*, which sank rapidly after being hit by as many as seven torpedoes, and the concrete quay Fox-6. Here a cutter fishes a survivor out the water alongside *West Virginia* at the edge of the burning oil. The ship has already settled on the bottom in an upright position. (USN)

2. The story of the attempted escape of *Nevada* was one of the most exciting of the day. Due to her position at the far north end of Ford Island, she was hit by only one torpedo, leaving her still seaworthy. Therefore, about 40 minutes after the attack began she got underway, heading along 'Battleship Row' towards the harbour entrance. This view from the control tower on Ford Island shows her alongside Ten-Ten Dock. She had to swing close to the far shore to clear a dredge working just ahead, off the right edge of this photograph. The small seaplane tender *Avocet* (AVP-4) is docked in the foreground. (USN)

▲33

33. It was at this moment, about 0850 hours, that *Nevada* began to attract the attention of the dive-bombers of the second wave. Five bombs struck the ship almost simultaneously, causing serious fires forward and at the base of the foremast. Now beginning to settle by the bow, she was ordered by Admiral Furlong, CO of the Fleet's minecraft but ranking officer on the scene, to head for the west side of Ford Island rather than try the entrance channel. (USN)

▼34

34. Having passed the dredge, connected to the shore by the pipeline seen in the middleground, *Nevada* continued only for a short distance before flooding at the bow forced her aground on the east shore of the channel adjacent to the dry dock where the destroyer *Shaw* (DD-373) was burning, contributing to the large cloud of black smoke behind *Nevada* in this view. *Avocet* is again in the foreground. (USN)

5. This location was totally unsatisfactory, as *Nevada* was now ↑locking the main exit from the East Loch of Pearl Harbor. Admiral ↑urlong again intervened, ordering two tugs to push *Nevada* away ↑om the east shore toward the shallower west side, and, accord-↑gly, two tugs began swinging *Nevada*'s stern around, pivoting on ↑er grounded bow. At the time this photograph was taken, approxi-↑ately 0930 hours, this process is about half complete. *Nevada*

stretches across the East Loch channel. (USN)

36. Having swung *Nevada* completely around, the tugs now began trying to pull her off the east shore, stern-first. Fortunately, this occurred without too much delay, as the ship was now taking water rapidly by the bow. *Shaw*, in the dry dock to the left, continues to burn furiously. (USN)

37. This view from the Gasoline Wharf along Ford Island shortly after 1000 hours shows *Nevada*, between the smoke from *Shaw* to the left and that from the seaplane hangars at the southern tip of Ford Island in the centre, being towed stern-first towards the western shore. *California*, to the right, is settling on the bottom. (USN)

◄38

39 ▲

38. Seen the next day over the partially burned-out seaplane facility at the southern tip of Ford Island, *Nevada* is now firmly resting on the shallow bottom near Waipio Point on the west shore of the main channel. (USN)

39. On the western side of Ford Island another drama was played out on 7 December. The old battleship (now target ship) *Utah* (AG-16), the old light cruisers *Detroit* (CL-8) and *Raleigh* (CL-7) and the seaplane tender *Tangier* (AV-8) occupied berths normally reserved for the Pacific Fleet's three aircraft carriers, which, fortunately for the Navy, were otherwise engaged that morning. What was lucky for the Navy was less of a blessing for the sailors on board two of the four ships docked along Ford Island's west side. *Utah* and *Raleigh* were both hit by torpedoes before the attackers turned their attention elsewhere. *Utah*, to the right in this view, capsized rapidly; *Raleigh* began to list and probably would have followed suit but for the quick action of a harbour tug that forced a barge alongside. Lashed in place, the barge provided the necessary stability and time for damage crews to save the ship. (USN)

40. The sad duty of searching for survivors began immediately. *Oklahoma* capsized so rapidly that a number of sailors were trapped inside; here salvage crews work desperately to save them. Altogether 32 men were freed from *Oklahoma* after she capsized, the last not being rescued until 9 December. *Maryland*, inboard of *Oklahoma*, was the least damaged of the battleships, receiving only one bomb hit. She was declared ready for action just eleven days after the raid. (USN)

40 ▼

▲41 ▼42

1. For the minimal US naval forces in the Western Pacific, the first months of the war were interesting, to say the least. Isolated and mostly without air cover, ships found movement near any of the battle zones very dangerous. Here *Peary* (DD-226) disappears behind splashes of bombs off Manila, 26 December 1941. She survived this encounter – but not for long, being sunk during the Port Darwin raid, 5 February 1942.

2. Another vessel that did not survive was the submarine *Sealion* (SS-193), which was caught by Japanese aircraft in dock undergoing repairs at Cavite. Over successive raids she was damaged and then finally sunk. This photograph showing *Sealion*'s remains appeared in a Japanese wartime publication dated May 1942. (USMC)

3, 44. Eventually, the only ships capable of re-supplying Wainwright's beleaguered garrisons on Bataan and Corregidor were submarines. They would pull into Manila Bay at dusk, fully loaded with food, ammunition and medical supplies, generally taking out casualties, civilian refugees or just sandbags as ballast. This latter became so precious that when *Trout* (SS-202) made one such supply run in February 1942, she was ballasted with a relatively less valuable cargo, the gold reserves of the Philippines Treasury. These photographs show *Trout*'s return to Pearl Harbor and part of the loot. Submarines were painted black overall during the first half of the war. (USN)

43 ▲ 44 ▼

▲45   ▼46

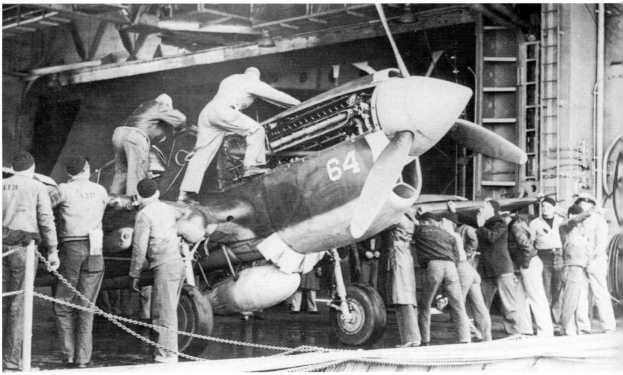

47▲

45. One of the few US ships in the Far East that survived was *Marblehead* (CL-12), and she paid a price. Caught by Japanese bombers north of Bali on 4 February 1942, she was damaged beyond the ability of any local yard to repair her, reaching port only by steering with her screws. This photograph was taken the next day at Tjilatjap and shows local labourers helping the crew to shore up the damaged areas at the stern. Perhaps this was a lucky wound because it led to her withdrawal to Australia, and she thus missed the Battle of the Java Sea on 27 February that saw the end of the remaining Allied naval forces in the Far East. (USN)

46. The early months of the war in the Atlantic differed from the 'short of war' period only in that the gloves were now off. The pitifully few carriers in the Atlantic were used for aircraft transport and to escort very high value convoys. *Ranger* (CV-4), seen here loading an Army P-40 on 14 April 1942, was used to escort the large troop convoy WS.10 from Britain to Bombay in late December 1941. This aircraft and 39 more like it were intended for the defence of India: they were carried across the South Atlantic and flown off to

Accra, whence they flew across Africa to India. (USN)

47. Another of the precious Atlantic Fleet carriers, *Wasp* (CV-7), in the company of HMS *Edinburgh* crossing the Atlantic en route to Britain in early April 1942. The photograph was taken from *Washington* (BB-56). On 14 April *Wasp* set off from Greenock as part of the Anglo-American Force 'W', escort for Operation 'Calendar', another of the Malta relief efforts. *Wasp* carried a load of 47 Spitfires which were flown off on 20 April; she was back at Scapa Flow on the 26th, having conducted the only sortie of an American fleet carrier into the Mediterranean during the Second World War. (USN)

48. *Washington* stayed at Scapa Flow, becoming part of a force of American naval units sent to relieve elements of the RN's Home Fleet which were needed for Operation 'Ironclad', the landings on Madagascar. *Washington* remained in British waters for over two months, becoming part of the distant cover force for the infamous convoy PQ.17. She is seen here in April 1942 at Scapa; HMS *Victorious* is in the foreground. (USN)

48▼

▲49   ▼50

49. Another member of the American delegation at Scapa in April 1942 was *Tuscaloosa* (CA-37), which remained in the Atlantic for the greater part of the war. She was part of the close cover force for PQ.17. The threat of a sortie by German surface forces led to the order for the withdrawal of the escort and dispersal of the convoy. The result was a disaster, 24 merchantmen being lost to the combined efforts of the *Luftwaffe* and U-boats. HMS *London* is in the background.

50. *Augusta* (CA-51), flagship of the Atlantic Fleet, 18 April 1942. This and the next three photographs offer a study in theme and variations on Measure 12 Mod. Derived from the three-colour, horizontally graded Measure 12, the modified scheme called for the edges of the bands to be made uneven. This initiated a period of fantastic invention as schemes were drawn up and applied as and when ships passed through East Coast dockyards. *Augusta*'s scheme is a very early example of the type. The three colours (Sea Blue,

Ocean Gray and Haze Gray) are still very obviously graded dark to light, with 'tongues' of each colour extending into adjacent areas. Being a flagship has some advantages: *Augusta*'s radar suite was the best then available, including the CXAM-1 on the foremast and a new FC fire control set just below. (NHC)

51. The scheme seen on *Wichita* (CA-45) on 22 April 1942 represents an average of complexity of Measure 12 Mod., with the 'tongues' of colour more irregular in shape and greater in number. *Wichita* remained in the Atlantic only for the early part of the war, but was joined by the replacement forces during 'Ironclad'. (USN)

52. The paint scheme on *Wasp* (CV-7), seen from HMS *Edinburgh* on 22 April 1942, shows yet another variation on the theme: the edges of the colour bands, at least on the hull, are more angular. *Wasp* is now returning from Operation 'Calendar' and her sortie into the Mediterranean. The aircraft on her deck are Douglas Devastators, part of her own air group. (USN)

▲ 53

53. An extreme of 'angularity' can be seen on *Lang* (DD-399), photographed off Hampton Roads from one of *Wasp*'s aircraft, 26 May 1942. This violated the spirit, if not the letter, of the Measure 12 regulations; it did, however, anticipate the angular schemes of the future, Measure 17 introduced later in 1942 and the well-known disruptive schemes (Measures 31, 32 and 33) that appeared in 1943. *Lang* had been part of *Wasp*'s escort for 'Calendar'; now, along with *Wasp*, she was heading for the South Pacific. (USN)

54. They also serve who only escort convoys. This relatively unglamorous duty was relegated to the oldest ships, such as the antique battleship *New York* (BB-34), seen in February 1942. Her radar is new, at least: she carries the recently introduced SC search radar, an improved CXAM-1, on her foretop, along with an FC antenna, and another FC antenna is sited on the after control position, just aft of the funnel. (USN)

▼ 54

55▲

55. A use was found for battleships considered too old even for escort duty. *Wyoming* (AG-17, ex-BB-32), launched in 1911, served as a gunnery training ship, providing invaluable practice for new recruits. In this June 1942 photograph she still has three main turrets and only a few AA guns. These would later proliferate, as on all US Navy ships. (USN)

56. The decisive weapon in the Battle of the Atlantic would be the escort carrier, emerging in unheard-of numbers from American shipyards. But that was off in the future: in mid-1942 there were just a handful, the busiest of which was still the original, *Long Island* (CVE-1). This photograph was taken almost exactly one year after the one seen earlier (photo 6). *Long Island* now had an extended flight deck and Measure 12 Mod. camouflage. The significance of her hull number, '751', remains a mystery. (USN)

56▼

▲ 57

57. Another Atlantic veteran was the light cruiser *Brooklyn* (CL-40), seen here from one of *Wasp*'s aircraft at Hampton Roads, 26 May 1942. *Brooklyn*, generally engaged in Atlantic and Mediterranean operations from September 1941 through to the end of the war, was one of only a small number of US warships not involved in the Pacific at some time during the conflict. (USN)

58. Underway refuelling is a tricky business in the best of circumstances, but in the stormy North Atlantic in winter it was always dangerous. Here *Woolsey* (DD-437) gets fuel from *Kaweah* (AO-15) during anti-submarine escort operations, 2 February 194 Like *Brooklyn*, *Woolsey* remained engaged in ASW in the Atlantic for the entire war. Note the absence of No. 1 turret. (USN)

▼ 58

9. A *Benson/Livermore* Class destroyer, in Measure 12 Mod., at sea the Atlantic, early 1942. The modified Measure 12 scheme took e three horizontally layered colours of the original measure (Sea lue, Ocean Gray and Haze Gray) and applied them in fluid plotches'. While these patterns were varied and may have seemed ndom, they were in fact carefully planned. Incidentally, hotograph 68 shows another destroyer in the identical camouflage attern. (USN)

60. Another Atlantic Fleet destroyer, this time an old First World War-vintage 'four-piper', in Measure 12 Mod. camouflage. This is a sharper photograph, clearly showing the three colours of the scheme. Horizontal surfaces are Deck Blue, a tone in the same purple-grey series as that used on the vertical surfaces. Despite the fact that it was darker than Sea Blue, Deck Blue nearly always appears lighter in photographs because of the greater reflection of light off horizontal surfaces. (USN)

61, 62. *Quincy* (CA-39), seen in the South Pacific in August 1942, wearing a faded Measure 12 Mod. scheme. The flags being aired out from the aft yardarm give a true reading of the colour balance of the first of these photographs, namely that it is slightly weak in blue, accounting for the neutral appearance of the hull colours which should have more of a blue cast. The second photograph shows the ship behind a troop transport, which is painted in Measure 11 or a very early Measure 21 overall Navy Blue scheme. Sea Blue and Navy Blue were very similar in appearance, the latter being somewhat darker. *Quincy* probably looked much the same during her Atlantic operations early in the war. She came to the South Pacific in June 1942 as part of the escort for *Wasp*. (USN)

3. After the devastation at Pearl Harbor, there was understandable confusion and misdirection in naval strategy in the Pacific. Three ill-advised single carrier raids against Japanese island targets were attempted, with minimal results, during the first months of 1942 before sanity returned to naval planning. The South Pacific was clearly going to be the major US theatre of operations during the war's opening phases: it was there that the Japanese still had ambitions and room to expand. The obvious first priority was the protection of the sea route to Australia, and, with that in mind, troop convoys were rapidly organized to bring garrisons to some of the essential waypoints on the route. One such was Bora Bora, part of the Society Island group that includes Tahiti. The old light cruiser *Trenton* (CL-11) was pressed into service as an escort for six troop-ships carrying 4,500 soldiers for Bora Bora that left Pearl Harbor on 31 January 1942. She is seen at her destination on 27 February. (USN)

64. *Richmond* (CL-9) was another old light cruiser used for escort duty on the Australia run in the early days of the war. She, too, is seen at Bora Bora in February 1942. Like *Trenton*, she wears a somewhat faded standard Measure 12 camouflage paint scheme. (USN)

▲65   ▼66

65–68. A quartet of Atlantic Fleet destroyers, all photographed off Hampton Roads by *Wasp*'s aircraft on 26 May 1942. Again, note the variations in the interpretation of the Measure 12 Mod. camouflage scheme. Photograph 65 shows *Trippe* (DD-403), a *Craven* Class destroyer which was part of *Ranger*'s escort to Bombay in December 1941. *Ingraham* (DD-444), photograph 66, belonged to the *Benson/Livermore* Class (Group 2); at the time, these were the most modern destroyers in the US Navy. *Sterett* (DD-407), photograph 67, was another *Craven* Class destroyer. Like *Lang* (photograph 53), she

came to the Atlantic Fleet from the Pacific in May 1941 and, after an active year in the Atlantic, was now returning to the Pacific Fleet as part of *Wasp*'s escort. Note the non-standard use of the darkest camouflage colour (Sea Blue) on the forward superstructure. *Edison* (DD-439), photograph 68, was another *Benson/Livermore*, and remained in the Atlantic throughout the war. Her camouflage pattern is identical to that seen on *Gleaves* (photograph 3). Despite the random appearance of the designs used, they obviously were painted to established patterns. (USN)

▲69

▲70　　▼71

40

69. Another element in the strategy to contain Japanese expansion into the South Pacific was the establishment of a mixed RN/RAN/USN cruiser force for escort and patrol duty in the Coral Sea and Fiji Basin. This and the next four photographs were taken at Suva, Fiji, in February 1942. This view shows HMS *Leander*, with the USN heavy cruiser *Chicago* (CA-29) nearly hidden behind. (USN)

70. *Leander* and *Chicago* again, this time with a yacht in between. The yacht could very well be one of the numerous such boats impressed into naval service to act as coastal patrol vessels. *Leander*'s 'splinter' camouflage scheme was typical of RN practice at the time; *Chicago*'s scheme appears to be the short-lived Measure 41, overall Sea Blue. (USN)

71. This multi-national cruiser unit went by various titles and its composition varied over time. Some of its members were more or less permanently assigned while others rotated in and out. *Leander*, for instance, was a temporary member, while *Chicago* and HMAS *Australia*, seen here, were permanent members. The force was under the command of the Australian Admiral Crace. (USN)

72, 73. A rather famous temporary member at this time was HMS *Achilles*, the veteran of action off the River Plate. Like *Leander*, she was no longer with Crace's force when, as TG.17.3, it took part in the Battle of the Coral Sea in early May 1942. The cruiser force was detached from the main carrier group on 7 May with orders to patrol the southern edge of the Louisades, guarding against the movement of Japanese troopships towards Port Moresby. (USN)

▲74 ▼75

74. US carrier forces had been busy since Pearl Harbor. After the ill-advised 'revenge raids' of the very early months of the war, a more rational policy was developed, although one more spectacular raid was still in the works. While *Yorktown* and *Lexington* were despatched to the South Pacific to guard against the anticipated next move by the Japanese, *Hornet* and *Enterprise* were sent with a load of USAAF B-25s under the command of Jimmy Doolittle to bomb Japan. Tactically the raid was meaningless and strategically it was a disaster because it diverted half of the available carrier forces in the Pacific away from the major theatre of operations, but the value to public confidence in striking a blow, even if only symbolic, against the Japanese capital was immeasurable. Here the two carriers, just back from the Tokyo Raid, are seen en route from Pearl Harbor to the South Pacific, 3 May 1942. They arrived too late for the Battle of the Coral Sea. (USN)

75. The Battle of the Coral Sea stretched over several days, the major action taking place on 8 May 1942 when the Japanese and American main carrier groups, *Shokaku* and *Zuikaku*, versus *Lexington* (CV-2) and *Yorktown* (CV-5), finally found each other. The Americans struck first, putting three bombs into *Shokaku*, damaging her flight deck to the point that she could no longer launch aircraft; *Zuikaku*, beneath a rain squall, was undamaged. The Japanese response was already in the air. *Yorktown* was hit by single bomb but was able to continue operations; *Lexington* bore the brunt of the attack. This photograph shows her from directly ahead at the height of the Japanese attack, twisting at high speed and with bombs falling off her starboard side. (NHC)

76, 77. The fate of an attacking Japanese 'Kate' carrier-based torpedo-bomber, which came in at low level over one of *Lexington*'s escorting destroyers. In photograph 76, the aircraft has been hit, and trails fire; the red *hinomaru* on her wings show up clearly in this shot, which was obviously taken with orthochromatic film. Photo 77 shows the 'Kate' splashing. The defence was tough but enough of the attackers got through to hit *Lexington* with two bombs and two torpedoes. These photographs, and most of those following, were taken from the cruiser *New Orleans* (CA-32), part of *Lexington*'s screen. (NHC)

76▲ 77▼

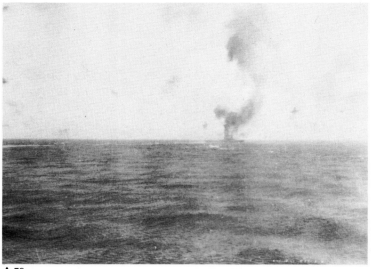

▲ 78

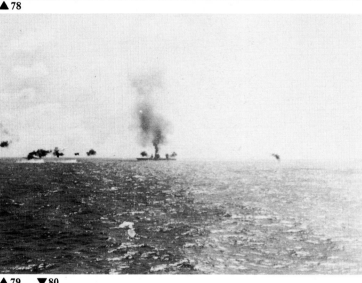

▲ 79 ▼ 80

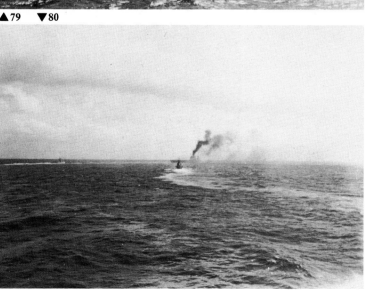

78, 79. The immediate effect of the Japanese attack was to leave *Lexington* dead in the water. In these views, taken minutes apart from opposite sides, she i drifting to a halt, venting huge clouds of smoke from a bomb hit at the base of her funnel but keeping up a rapid and largely effective anti-aircraft fire. Even from a distance, it is possible to tell that she is listing to port and is down at the bow. (NHC)

80. The air attack over, escorting destroyers rush to the aid of the stricken *Lexington*. The damage from the bombs and torpedoes was diagnosed as being less serious than originally feared. Although three stubborn fires continued to burn below decks, her powerplant and hull were basically intact and counterflooding soon had her once again on an even keel. (NHC)

81. So optimistic was the prognosis for the patient that *Lexington* was soon making 24kts again and was able to recover her air group when it returned about an hour after the Japanese attack. Nevertheless, the ship is noticeably down by the bow and her air group had to be spotted on the deck rather than being struck below because of the persistent fires still burning below decks. Her camouflage is Measure 11 overall Sea Blue, common on Pacific Fleet ships during a brief period in early 1942. (NHC)

82, 83. Conditions on board *Lexington* deteriorated a the morning passed, and by noon it was becoming obvious that the fires below were not being controlle by the crew's efforts. These views show *Lexington*'s flight deck forward and aft at about this time. Work parties continue to repair the damage caused by the bomb that hit the flight deck forward while fire-fighting teams stand around with little to do. Aft, a few crewmen move between the Wildcats and Dauntlesses of CVG-2, wary of the smoke rising around the edges of the aft centreline lift. (USN/NHC)

81▲

82▲   83▼

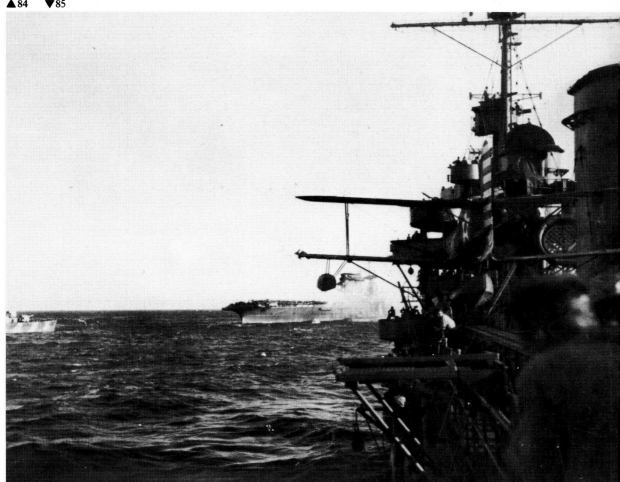

4. At 1247 hours the fires below decks reached avgas fumes leaking rom ruptured storage tanks, resulting in the first of two huge xplosions that destroyed *Lexington*'s ventilation system and spread re throughout the ship. This illustration shows *Lexington* shortly ter the second explosion, at about 1400 hours. The fires are now mpletely out of control and the marked list to port has returned. HC)

5–87. By 1600 the fires had forced the evacuation of the machinery aces and led to the decision to abandon ship. The escort force, nder the command of Rear-Admiral Kinkaid, skilfully handled the rescue of the crew. The first photograph was again taken from *New Orleans* as she approaches *Lexington*'s port quarter. Note the SOC seaplane on the cruiser's port catapult. In the second view, one of *Lexington*'s escort of four *Sims* Class destroyers is seen pulled up alongside. It is almost hidden in the thin smoke still pouring from the carrier's fires. In photograph 87, a heavily laden launch carries survivors from one of the escort destroyers towards the more commodious cruiser. The reduced volume of smoke does not reflect the true state of *Lexington*'s fires. (NHC)

87▼

▲88

88. A close-up view of *Lexington*'s stern shows crewmen sliding down ropes as they abandon ship. Waiting launches picked them up almost as soon as they hit the water. So orderly was the evacuation that 150 wounded crewmen were lowered in basket stretchers directly into the arms of waiting rescuers. (USN)

89. Two of *Lexington*'s escort destroyers wait patiently astern of

their dying charge. *Morris* (DD-417) is in the foreground; her partner is another member of the *Sims* class, one of *Anderson* (DD-411), *Hammann* (DD-412) or *Russell* (DD-414). They are still painted in the Measure 12 Mod. scheme they carried back from the Atlantic, where they were employed in the first days of the war. All guns still point skywards, in case the Japanese return. (USN)

▼89

48

. One cruiser, either *New Orleans* or *Minneapolis* (CA-36), and
~~t~~ree of *Lexington*'s four escorting destroyers are seen here late in
~~th~~e afternoon of 8 May 1942 as the rescue of the carrier's crew was
~~su~~ccessfully completed. At 2000, fearful that Japanese surface
~~fo~~rces might capture the smouldering wreck it was ordered that she
~~be~~ torpedoed – a sad end for a noble lady. (USN)

.. The sorrowful duty of scuttling *Lexington* fell to *Phelps* (DD-

360), seen here at Pearl Harbor between the times of Coral Sea and
Midway. As soon as the sun set on 8 May *Yorktown* and her escorts
(including *Phelps*) headed back to Noumea and thence directly to
Pearl Harbor at best speed. Haste was called for: intelligence was
indicating that another, even bigger Japanese operation was in the
works, this one aimed due east. (USN)

▲92 ▼93

94 ▲

92–94. In the last two weeks of May 1942 Pearl
Harbor was again frantic with activity as ships arrived
from the South Pacific, were repaired and
provisioned and were despatched to one of the two
carrier task forces forming up at sea near Midway or
the cruiser force in the Aleutians: the Navy was not
going to get caught in harbour again. Photograph 92
shows *Dewey* (DD-349), another veteran of Coral
Sea, leaving port to join TG.16.4, the escort for
Enterprise and *Hornet* off Midway. Like most other
Pacific Fleet vessels, she wears Measure 11.
Photograph 93 shows the heavy cruiser *New Orleans*
(CA-32) passing through Pearl Harbor, late May
1942. She joined TG.16.5 off Midway. *Astoria* (CA-
34), seen lowering a launch in photograph 94, had
been part of *Yorktown*'s escort at Coral Sea and would
serve the same function at Midway. (USN)

▲95

95. Intelligence also pinpointed
the Aleutian Islands as a likely
target of the Japanese, and so a
cruiser force, TF.8 under
'Fuzzy' Theobald, was
assembled and despatched to
protect Dutch Harbor.
Louisville (CA-28), seen here at
the beginning of 1942, was
assigned to TF.8. At the time,
she still wore Measure 1.
(NHC)

96. *St. Louis* (CL-49) at Pearl
Harbor, May 1942. She, too,
was assigned to TF.8 for duty in
the Aleutians. In May and June
the weather in the Aleutians is
terrible, with sudden wind
storms and dense ice fogs, and
TF.8, composed of five cruisers
and their accompanying
destroyers, was unable to
interfere with Japanese attacks
on Dutch Harbor or the
invasion of Attu and Kiska.
(USN)

97. *Enterprise* (CV-6), along
with *Hornet* (CV-8), had rushed
to the South Pacific in late April
1942 but had arrived too late for
Coral Sea. Now the carriers
were rushed back again to Pearl
Harbor for a quick resupply
before heading out again
towards Midway. This battle
they would not miss. *Enterprise*
is seen here at Pearl Harbor,
painted in Measure 11; note the
CXAM-1 radar on her foretop.
(NHC)

96▲   97▼

▲ 98   ▼ 99

98, 99. Newly arrived from the Atlantic, the veteran cruiser *Vincennes* (CA-44, above) and the new *Atlanta* (CL-51, left) are seen at Pearl Harbor in late May 1942, also sporting Measure 12 Mod. paint schemes. Both ships were assigned to TG.16.2, the escort for *Enterprise* and *Hornet*. *Atlanta* was the lead ship of a class of dedicated AA light cruisers, intended specifically to protect carriers from air attack. Essentially, she was an over-sized destroyer with a flush-deck design and eight twin 5in dual-purpose turrets. The careers of both the ships in the Pacific would be exciting but brief: by the end of the year both would be sunk off Guadalcanal. (USN)

100. *Hornet* at Pearl Harbor between the Battles of the Coral Sea and Midway. The Measure 12 camouflage she brought from the Atlantic is still intact, and the apparent deterioration along the waterline is actually a very complex attempt at a fake bow wave (Measure 5), intended to create a false impression of speed. (USN)

▲101

101. *Pensacola* (CA-24), the oldest active heavy cruiser in the US Navy, also passed through Pearl Harbor at this time; she too was on her way to join TG.16.5. Note the CXAM radar, the experimental model that preceded the CXAM-1. (USN)

102. *Yorktown* (CV-5) also rushed back to Pearl Harbor from the South Pacific. She was given a triumphal welcome, with her crew lining the flight deck in their dress whites. Unlike the other two carriers, *Yorktown* had battle damage to attend to, from one bomb hit and several near-misses at Coral Sea. The dockyard engineers estimated that three months would be required for her repair. Nimitz gave them forty-eight hours. (NHC)

103. Incredibly, the schedule was met. *Yorktown* was dry-docked as soon as she arrived, and within two days she was sailing towards Midway. She is still painted in a 'straight' Measure 12, with horizontal bands of colour, and, like *Pensacola*, she carries the experimental CXAM radar, seen end-on in this view. (NASM)

104. The Battle of Midway would mark the dramatic and sudden stemming of the tide of Japanese advances. Four Japanese aircraft

carriers, the bulk of the striking force, would go down to fiery deaths within a day, but not without exacting a price. By intelligence, skill and luck, American dive-bombers found themselves over the Japanese fleet shortly after 1020 hours on 4 June 1942. Having attacked Midway Atoll, the Japanese commander Nagumo had vacillated for too long about whether to send his remaining aircraft against Midway or the American fleet. He eventually chose to attack the American carriers, but this required changing the armament of the aircraft still on board and the hasty recovery, refuelling and re-arming of the Midway strike force. The US dive-bombers crashed into decks filled with fuelled and armed aircraft, and within minute three of the Japanese carriers were doomed. Only *Hiryu*, separated from the rest, survived this devastation to launch its own strike at the Americans. The victim was to be *Yorktown*, seen here just before *Hiryu*'s first strike arrived at about 1400. She has her air group back on board, waiting for *Hiryu* to be found. (USN)

▼102

103▲ 104▼

▲105 ▼106

105. The first attack was by a pitifully small force of eighteen 'Jill' dive-bombers, and *Yorktown*'s combat air patrol got nearly all the attackers. Only three enemy aircraft broke through, but they planted all their bombs on *Yorktown*, starting fires among her aircraft and at the base of her funnel. (USN)

106. While fires still burned at the base of *Yorktown*'s funnel, repair crews began trying to restore the integrity of the ship's flight deck forward so that undamaged aircraft could be pushed out of the way. Note the arresting cables across the deck forward. Early US carriers were equipped to land aircraft over the bow in case the aft end of the flight deck was damaged, but in practice this was rarely done. (NASM)

107. A welder (foreground) waits his turn while carpenters' mates chop away at the splintered boards around a bomb hole in *Yorktown*'s deck. Unlike those of British carriers, the flight decks of US carriers, up until the last class of the war, were unarmoured, being composed of thin steel sheet covered with thick wood planks. The welder is here just to cut any protruding metal out of the way, so that the carpenters can cover the hole with new planks. (NASM)

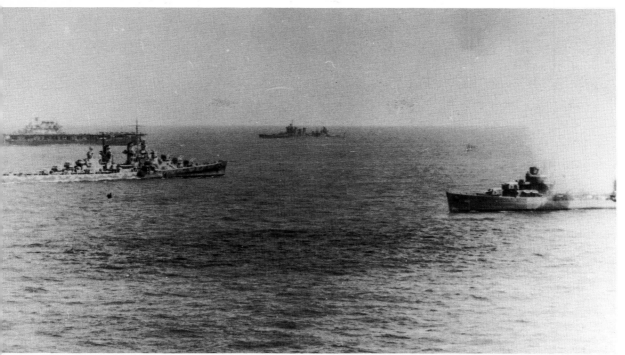

◀108
109▲

108. There are always spectators! Idle crewmen manning the
director and two 1.1in AA mounts at the after end of *Yorktown*'s
island watch the fire-fighters and repair crews. Note the large
aircraft handling crane with its boom swung into the stowed
position on the outboard side of the island. The quadruple 1.1in AA
gun proved too slow and difficult to train and lacked the punch to
make it an effective medium AA weapon. (USN)
109. *Yorktown* and her escorts soon after the first attack. The carrier
has stopped while her fire-fighters bring the last of the fires under

control. Her escort seen in this view includes, from the left, the AA
light cruiser *Atlanta*; either *New Orleans* or *Minneapolis*; and the
destroyer *Phelps*. (USN)
110. In this photograph, taken seconds later, *Phelps* is seen belching
white smoke, although, despite appearances, she proved not to have
been damaged – she simply ran out of fuel in the excitement of the
Japanese attack. She was soon replenished, and she rejoined
Yorktown's screen. (USN)

110▼

▲111

111. The fires on *Yorktown* were soon extinguished. Here, just before the second attack, she appears to be steaming normally again, with the remnants of her air group pushed forward on her flight deck. The second attack was by ten of *Hiryu's* 'Kate' torpedo-bombers arriving at 1445. Again, most of the attackers were shot down, but two got through and put torpedoes into *Yorktown's* port side. (USN)

112. The two torpedoes left *Yorktown* listing rapidly to port and cut all power in the ship. When the list reached 26 degrees in only fifteen minutes, the captain, aware that his ship's watertight integrity was suspect after the near-misses she survived at Coral Sea

and afraid that she might be capsizing, gave the order to abandon ship. (NHC)

113. A water-damaged photograph of the scene on *Yorktown's* flight deck after the second attack. Crewmen congregate alongside the island, instinctively seeking what stability they can on the listing deck. (NASM)

114. Escorts again mill around *Yorktown* as her crew abandon ship; *Vincennes* steams between the photographer and the carrier. One of the escorting destroyers, from the same squadron of *Sims* Class vessels that stood by at *Lexington's* sinking, swings in close to *Yorktown's* stern to begin picking up survivors. (NHC)

▼112

113▲ 114▼

▲115

115. The same destroyer is seen now along *Yorktown*'s starboard side as crewmen slide down ropes to waiting cutters. *Yorktown* proved to be a lot tougher than her captain imagined, however: she floated for 24 hours with no crew on board until, concluding that she might indeed be saved, a skeleton crew was put back to restart her pumps and she was taken in tow. (NHC)

116. Her survival was just not in the stars: under tow on 6 June, she was hit by two torpedoes from the Japanese submarine *I-68*. While her escort searched for the attacker her list again increased and she began to settle. (NHC)

117. Again, *Yorktown* was abandoned, her small salvage crew being evacuated uneventfully. Here a launch from one of her screening destroyers patrols forlornly along her port side looking for any stragglers. (USN)

▼116

▲118

▲119 ▼120

118. Five escorts (one virtually hidden behind *Yorktown*) wait as the big carrier sinks. While a fitting tribute to a gallant ship, this death watch was to prove to be ill-advised. (NHC)

119. *I-68* claimed one more victim that day. In the same attack that doomed *Yorktown*, the submarine managed to put a torpedo into *Hammann* (DD-412), which sank in four minutes, taking 81 of her crew with her. (NHC)

120. Survivors meet at Midway after the battle as the heavy cruiser *Pensacola* (CA-24) disembarks reinforcements for the Marine garrison on Sand Island 25 June 1942. In the foreground is the wreckage of the sole surviving TBF out of the small detachment of VT-8 Avengers that flew against the Japanese fleet. *Pensacola* now has an FC fire control radar on her foretop, just beneath the tilted CXAM air search set. (USN)